THE A, B & C of Democracy

THE A, B & C of Democracy

(or cats in the sack)

LUCA BELGIORNO-NETTIS
& KYLE REDMAN

CARLOW BOOKS

Published by Carlow Books,
an imprint of Schwartz Books Pty Ltd
Level 1, 221 Drummond Street
Carlton VIC 3053, Australia
enquiries@blackincbooks.com
www.blackincbooks.com

Copyright © Luca Belgiorno-Nettis and Kyle Redman 2021
Luca Belgiorno-Nettis and Kyle Redman assert their right to be known
as the authors of this work.

ALL RIGHTS RESERVED.
No part of this publication may be reproduced, stored in a retrieval system,
or transmitted in any form by any means electronic, mechanical, photocopying,
recording or otherwise without the prior consent of the publishers.

9781760643379 (paperback)
9781743822104 (ebook)

A catalogue record for this
book is available from the
National Library of Australia

Cover design by John Warwicker
Text design and typesetting by Typography Studio

Contents

*   *   *

'I would say the greatest challenge of our time is to find ways to enable democratic citizens to be citizens—to learn how to reason together about what makes for a just society. And we have precious few places and resources for this.'[1]

Michael Sandel
Anne T. and Robert M. Bass Professor of Government Theory,
Harvard University

Acknowledgements

Much of this book draws on the work done by Iain Walker and Kyle Redman, Executive Director and Program Manager respectively of The newDemocracy Foundation, in writing the original United Nations Democracy Fund (UNDEF) handbook titled *Beyond Elections*. We're especially grateful to Annika Savill, Executive Head UNDEF, for trusting us with this project.

There were also numerous contributors, and newDemocracy thanks Claudia Chwalisz, Enkhtsetseg Dagva, David Farrell, Nicole Hunter, Josh Lerner, Jane Mansbridge, Roy Mayega, Beth Novek, Thamy Pogrebinschi, Graham Smith, Mark Warren and Jay Weatherill.

We thank Luca's fellow board directors, Lyn Carson and Kathy Jones, who have helped sustain newDemocracy from its beginnings in 2007. Luca's wife, Anita, is thanked for enduring the author. We also thank the *Russell Mills Foundation*, and Alex Mills in particular, for patiently and generously supporting this publication; and Morry Schwartz for helping us get to the finishing line.

Foreword

Today, governments the world over are under pressure from below. The digital revolution has turbo-charged connectivity and information way beyond what was possible with print, radio and television. Today, everyone is a publisher, empowered to have a say.

If the primary task of the legislature is to aggregate and align the multiplicity of voices, that alignment is frustrated in our representative democracies: adversarial, short-term and poll-driven.

As governments continue to disappoint, there's a hankering for more effective models. In 2018, we were approached by the United Nations Democracy Fund to undertake a *Beyond Elections* project in three developing countries. The project was designed to demonstrate an alternative to the traditional processes of public policy development. We were also commissioned to produce a manual – the basis for this book – to provide practical guidance for those interested in doing democracy better. We thank you for your interest here, now.

Geoff Gallop AC, Chair

Nick Greiner AC, Deputy Chair

Research Committee of The newDemocracy Foundation

Introduction

I N 2020 WE SAW HOW THE US ELECTION generated an antagonistic political campaign. It's the new normal – America is not alone: elections everywhere deliver the same experience. The wisdom of the crowd may be exalted on election day but it's an oxymoron – that wisdom is little more than public opinion. Public opinion rewards the persuasiveness of spin, and spin reaches its nadir during political campaigns.

We don't need to be stuck in a rut that incites acrimonious and shallow politics. By toning down the vehemence, citizens' assemblies can act as a beacon for considered public discourse. By adding the voice of everyday people – beyond elections, political parties, lobbyists and campaign funding – we can deliberate together amicably, and agree about what is fair.

Inserted into this 'handbook' are three travel anecdotes – highlights from Luca's personal political journey around the world. The three diary entries – A, B & C – tell a story of global enthusiasm for a promising new future for democracy. In 2015, at the instigation of Luca's fellow director Professor Lyn Carson, newDemocracy established an international network of like-minded academics and practitioners: Democracy R&D[2]. At the time of print, the network boasts 89 members, in 30 countries on six continents.

The focus of the work is the 'minipublic', popularly known as citizens' juries or citizens' assemblies. It's when a democratic lottery is used to select a diverse group of people, representative in age, gender, geography and education, who are provided with the time and space to deliberate together. In Australia, we make regular use of juries. Our criminal juries are made up of people picked at random – in a civic lottery – who are then tasked with hearing a range of evidence for several days or weeks. Together, they discuss what they learn, who they trust and who they don't trust, and, if they're able to find common ground, reach a judgement. That's public judgement. The criminal jury is not a perfect example of a minipublic, but it's not a bad analogy. Selection by-lot satisfies an essential democratic principle – representation – and produces a fairer mix of people than any other method.

Involving a mix of everyday people in public decisions requires a certain formula. For starters, participation in a minipublic is not obligatory, as it is in a jury. People have busy lives, and not everyone can take the time to immerse themselves in detailed public policy issues, and spend their weekends resolving differences. People need to know their involvement will be meaningful. Participating is pointless if a decision has already been made. There needs to be the right incentives. When people are invited to help solve a problem, rather than being sold a solution, they're more likely to want to get involved. The combination of civic lottery and a meaningful opportunity to contribute generates the 'right' mix of people willing to give up their time for the public good.

Typically, our political leaders learn about what the public thinks through opinion polls, fleeting interviews and surveys, or, at best, a day-long focus group. In these circumstances, the participants have little time to reflect, and tend to react in ways that confirm their prior beliefs, or news commentary they've recently heard. A more informed understanding of the issue can expose what level of tolerance the public has for change, and can improve the democratic process fundamentally.

Whatever the public decision, the ideal outcome is one that has the informed support of the broader community. Take criminal justice, a recurring and contentious topic. If politicians don't support tough laws, they're accused of being 'asleep on the job and not protecting kids and families'. Beef up the laws, and they're attacked for 'running a police state and infringing civil liberties'. You can't win. If governments are open to any solution, they'll benefit from sharing the problem with the community. There is no *right* decision, just one that the public sees as *fair*.

For this book, we have three audiences in mind. First, you may be in elected office and feeling pressured by public opinion or social media campaigns. Powerful special interest groups are claiming to speak for the public, and it's hard to make compromises. You're faced with an electoral backlash – and 'realpolitik' – tough decisions are watered down or simply not taken. Second, you may be in the public service, and you want to consult with the community in a meaningful way. You want the community to be involved in the decisions that impact their lives, but you know that their five-minute view and their 40-hour view are different. Third, you may simply be interested in politics, and how it could be made better. You're wondering why it is that our political institutions are much older than many aspects of our modern society, and yet demonstrate much less innovation.

Public judgement is the outcome of many hours of dialogue and reflection. It's hard to believe a large group of complete strangers can actually do this, but they do. This handbook seeks to capture the learnings from more than 30 of newDemocracy's minipublics, and those of our many colleagues here and abroad.

1

What Is a Minipublic?

THE TERM 'MINIPUBLIC' DESCRIBES an assembly of the population in miniature. We achieve this by way of democratic lottery, which is how the Ancient Greeks constituted one of their most important law-making bodies: the Athenian Council. Most of us understand that selection by-lot is quintessentially representative, but when referring to the historic precedent we often hear the criticism: 'The Greeks didn't include women or slaves!' We acknowledge this, but after more than a hundred years of the universal franchise, true representation still hasn't been delivered. Modern electoral democracies are dominated by career politicians – mostly men – and don't readily accommodate women or people of low socio-economic status. Democratic lotteries do, since their sole purpose is to ensure that those inside the room look like those outside: a mirror image of the broader population.

Nevertheless, arguments against democratic lotteries persist, mostly concerning questions of meritocracy and competency. How can 'randoms' possibly make an intelligent contribution to difficult issues of public policy? There's ample evidence that they can, as highlighted by the 2020 OECD *Deliberative Wave* report[3]. If there's one thing that we hope to impart in this handbook, it's this: everyday people are more than capable of coming to informed conclusions about complex matters. The only proviso is that they need the time and space to do so.

Another common criticism is that because people are free to decide whether to accept an invitation or not, the mix of participants skews towards those sympathetic to 'government', appealing to 'progressives' rather than 'conservatives'. The argument is that the self-employed, for example, aren't interested or don't have time to participate. But one could say the same for the wage-earner. Our experience is that the real task in random selection is to reach and attract precisely those people who wouldn't normally respond: the least available and the least enthusiastic. Several incentives are needed to attract the otherwise disinterested, and we find that the most alluring carrot is the opportunity to meaningfully influence public policy.

When public comments or submissions are called for by governments, it's usual that the most invested people reply, and governments are often obliged to listen to these most insistent voices. These advocates also tend to come in pairs – with completely opposing positions – and normally it's very hard to make each happy. This is typically the job of governments – they do this all the time, but with mixed results. Parliaments, and the parliamentary committees charged with such hearings, are too often derailed by obvious political positioning. Introducing a group of everyday people – and not just elected officials – is a way to publicly demonstrate that all voices are given a fair hearing. A minipublic gives governments the chance to discover where the actual common ground is – a perspective absent from so much of the political dialogue today. By presenting the calm position of the general public, there's an opportunity to navigate through the stand-offs, the public opinion and wishlisting. This is both good policy and good politics.

It's very helpful to bring the media into the process early on, as journalists can share the story with the wider public. Since the use of minipublics is still uncommon, most journalists are intrigued to learn more. The 'people like me' angle does resonate with a broad readership.

A considerable amount of time is required to properly undertake a minipublic. Participants usually require about forty hours of meetings, spread out over more than a week, to become sufficiently informed and come to agreement. People are only satisfied when they've considered a range of information sources, discussed perspectives with one another and settled on recommendations. Situations where decisions must be made very quickly do not suit this process.

Deliberative processes are about common-ground agreement, and they can be jeopardised when placed in the spotlight of an entrenched political stand-off. The additional political pressure can make it difficult to patiently and appropriately consider all sides of an argument and reach agreement. Rushing a process, introducing it late or narrowing the scope can all look like attempts to massage a particular result. If stakeholders interpret it this way, it makes the process untenable. Participants immediately see this as well, and the entire project loses credibility, undermining any effort to share the problem.

On occasions where the window of time may not be ideal, it may be possible to make adjustments to the scope or scale of the questions asked of the group. For example, if a decision has already been made to build an airport, the scope can be constrained to how or where it should be built. By reducing the scope of the question, the group can focus on a specific trade-off, rather than start from the bigger question of whether or not an airport is needed.

Difficult or complex issues that require long-term thinking and strategic trade-offs are usually best suited to a long deliberative process. The catch is that governments must acknowledge that they cannot shape the final set of recommendations. Decision-makers must also be prepared to respond to – not necessarily endorse – all possible recommendations. If the government cannot accept this, then there's no alternative but to limit the remit or abandon the process.

Topic selection is where it begins. Openly describing the problem kicks off the conversation around how to find a solution, which is different from presenting a possible solution and only receiving feedback on that one option. Rather than asking people what services they would like, it's better to frame the question around the difficult task of making trade-off decisions. For example, rather than 'What services do you want from your water utility?', it's better to ask: 'We need to find a balance between price and service which is fair for everyone – how should we do this?' The second example clearly shares the problem, balancing costs and services. The first neglects the trade-off in favour of giving the participants a chance to create a wish list of what they want, which ultimately is not very useful information for costings.

'Where are the edges of the box?' is a query to be asked at the outset of any minipublic. What is the scope of the decision and what influence can the process have? These jurisdictional and authority questions need to be answered from the beginning. If the issue is contentious, there may need to be a process around agreeing on the scope. In a situation like this, the participants may be asked: 'This is the remit – can you live with it?' This can be useful in setting the boundaries on what the group considers. Any jurisdictional constraints should be resolved by providing absolute clarity and setting expectations about what can or cannot happen.

For example, a project in a local government area in Victoria asked participants for 'practical recommendations' on the structure of their council. There were some immediate changes that could be immediately implemented through regulation. Anything that went beyond this scope was considered an 'aspirational' change, requiring the government to pass new legislation. This allowed the deliberation to be channelled into two different streams: Practical and Aspirational. This was useful in opening up the decision, while also ensuring a focus on what was immediately possible.

Some decisions will impact an entire state or country, and so need to include people from all over, not just those in major cities. If there's major infrastructure spending for the state, then the jury must include people from regional and rural areas. National conversations will almost always include more than one group of participants to capture the experiences and descriptiveness of the entire country. How many groups, and where, will depend on the problem and how differently it manifests across the country.

The commitment from political authority impacts the level of diligence invested by the participants. Some decisions overlap with different departments or agencies, requiring all department heads to be onboard. It's usual to expect the government to respond to each recommendation. A clear public record of the government's response places enough weight on the citizens' work, and also shows that the government cannot simply discard the final report. Besides, the more the participants see that their decisions will be at least listened to – and not be consumed by the bureaucracy or ignored – the more seriously they will devote themselves to the deliberative process.

If politicians can make an upfront commitment to implement the recommendations, that's fantastic! However, that rarely happens. It's quite understandable that elected parliaments and councils have the ultimate prerogative for public policy. In any case, the responses to the recommendations should be a transparent explanation of how the government understands, rejects, or plans to modify or implement any recommendations. If, for whatever reason, the government intends to diverge from the recommendations or disagrees with them, it must make a public explanation as to why – or face the criticism of not listening to informed community members. Anything short of an assurance by government to provide a public response risks it being seen as dismissive.

An even better government response could be to establish an institutional role for everyday people in public decision-making – as we shall see in 'B Is for Belgium'.

A

A Is for Athens

THE VENUE IS THE ATHENS PRESIDENTIAL Mansion, and the occasion is the opening address at the 2017 *New York Times* Athens Democracy Forum. David Van Reybrouck and I are in lounge suits, whilst the six-foot-six moustached presidential guards are dressed in white pleated skirts and wear shoes with black pom-poms. We enjoy cocktails whilst mingling with delegates, former heads of state and well-known journalists.

David is a celebrity author in his own right, having published the bestselling *Congo: The Epic History of a People* in 2010. He has been invited to speak on the strength of a more recent book, *Against Elections: The Case for Democracy*.[4] More than 200 guests are then ushered into the grand ballroom, where we first hear from Prokopis Pavlopoulos, the Greek president, who delivers a fascinating but too lengthy and didactic monologue . . . in Greek, with no translators. We remain courteous, anxious for it to finish. Next comes

Kofi Annan, the former UN Secretary-General, and I feel some relief when he begins speaking in English. Halfway through his homily, which seems to be taking a familiar aristocratic arc, David and I are dumbstruck.

'We need to make our democracies more inclusive,' Annan says. 'This requires bold and innovative reforms to bring the young, the poor and minorities into the political system. An interesting idea put forward by one of your speakers this week, Mr Reybrouck, would be to reintroduce the Ancient Greek practice of selecting parliaments by-lot instead of election. In other words, parliamentarians would no longer be nominated by political parties, but chosen at random for a limited term, in the way many jury systems work. This would prevent the formation of self-serving and self-perpetuating political classes disconnected from their electorates.'[5]

David and I are ecstatic! Who has briefed him? Neither of us. After the speech, we grab Kofi for a selfie. We then seek out his assistant, Sebastian, and ask how Kofi came across *Against Elections*. 'I picked it up in a bookshop,' he says, 'and I inserted the idea into Mr Annan's speech.' Whatever – David and I remain jubilant. Having Kofi Annan promote the jury model to this audience, and in our presence, feels like a defining moment.

There's much we can learn from Ancient Athens. The distinctive genius of the Athenians was that their democracy included all men, rich and poor, and they selected their Council by democratic lottery, not by elections.

Earlier, before the speeches, with an appetiser and drink in hand, I had managed to waylay Annika Savill, the executive head of the United Nations Democracy Fund, and harangue her about the jury model. I'd already corresponded with her leading up to the event. She was unmoved then, as she was now. However, following Annan's speech, she pulls me aside and asks, 'How did Kofi hear of this?' And so begins our relationship with UNDEF – which has led to this handbook.

Two thousand years before male suffrage was granted to the propertied class in the United Kingdom and the United States of America, the Athenians had a completely different understanding of democracy. The Athenian Council (the Boule) was made up of 500 male citizens chosen by-lot. The Boule regularly proposed agendas for the Assembly, which was open to all male citizens, who gathered in a field below the acropolis. After arguments were presented, the Assembly voted on the issues.

George Tridimas, from Ulster University, writes:

With public office inconsequential for political influence, ambitious individuals who in modern times would have joined political parties to pursue their ideological causes could do so by winning Assembly votes. These observations go a long way to explain the small number of ancient references to elections, and the complete absence of references to today's ubiquitous office of prime minister or president. Individuals could propose their favourite measures directly to the Assembly, or ask one of the active political leaders to promote its cause. The right of any citizen to propose a policy opened agenda setting to all.[6]

Even though most people understand Athens to be the birthplace of democracy, there is little appreciation that elections for candidates did not feature at all. Policy measures were voted on, and were never entangled with the careers of ambitious politicians, as they are today. Some months after the Athens Democracy Forum, the *New York Times* runs a stinging review of *Against Elections*:

Van Reybrouck is a skilled polemicist, but his solutions to remedy 'democratic fatigue syndrome' are naïve and unfeasible. Echoing the Ancient Greek practice of drawing lots, he suggests replacing the

American House of Representatives with a random sample of citizens, like a jury pool. That seems like an utterly impractical way to govern nowadays and reflects the same demonization of political experience that led the country to favour a reality television star over a former secretary of state in 2016.

Van Reybrouck fetishizes direct democracy, like citizens' councils, but ignores the way existing electoral institutions could be made more responsive to the popular will through reforms like proportional representation or nonpartisan redistricting. The solution to democratic fatigue syndrome is to make elections more democratic, not to get rid of them altogether.[7]

David responds:

My book is a plea to enrich the current electoral model of representative democracy. Your reviewer laments this as 'naïve and unfeasible', but seems unaware of recent developments across the globe. What your reviewer considers 'utterly impractical' has helped Ireland resolve marriage equality. This type of citizen participation was also realized in South Australia to decide on the disposition of nuclear waste, a topic too toxic for party politics and too divisive for a referendum. Today cities like

Toronto, Madrid and Gdansk are even turning to civic lotteries as a permanent feature of their political landscape.[8]

In 2011, David established the Belgium G-1000 do-tank, and in 2018, guided the process to bring about the world's first permanent Citizens' Council in Belgium – as we shall see in 'B Is for Belgium'.

2

From Remit to Response

HANDING YOUR MOST COMPLICATED public decisions to a group of strangers, all equally likely to have come from the pub or the theatre, or to have worked on a construction site, in a lab or behind a desk during the week, can sound like a daunting prospect. Yet each of us in our everyday lives uses what Nobel Prize winner Daniel Kahneman and his colleague Amos Tversky famously termed 'slow thinking'.[9] We might be deciding on which phone to purchase, which job we want to pursue or where to go for a holiday. When we do this, we take our time, weigh information and determine what we think is the best course of action. We might ask our friends and family, who might help us to see things from a different perspective; we are sometimes motivated by our longer-term wellbeing, in contrast to our immediate satisfaction. We do this as a society as well. It's called good government. To do it well, we need to think about who is included, how they meet and what issue they address.

We've spoken a little about the *who* and the *how*. The *what* is the topic or remit. Having decided that an issue requires public deliberation, it then helps to think about the question. What do we want to ask of our citizens? What part of the issue can a deliberation by a minipublic influence? The chosen words need to be sufficiently expansive, but not so wide-ranging that participants are sidetracked into irrelevant discussions. If the remit is too narrow, it will confine the group's deliberations, and participants will understandably demand an explanation: 'Why are we being confined to only this aspect?'

Let's commence by defining the problem. What's the problem that needs to be solved? For example, increasing bus fares may be the specific issue at hand, but the underlying problem might be how we should pay for public transport. Be honest and focus on the real issue.

A good remit saves time. Here's an example from a project with limited time that necessitated a focused remit: 'The government is drafting a Gender Equality Bill. The setting of quotas is a key part of this. What quotas are fair? How can they be best implemented?' In this case, it's clearly stated that the government has already made the decision that a Gender Equality

Bill will be developed. This limits the scope of the process, clarifying for participants what they should spend their time on: namely, the nature and implementation of quotas, and not whether or not we should have a Gender Equality Bill.

A good remit will also allude to constraints that have been encountered. Here's an example of a remit for a water utility that worked well and included a trade-off: 'We need to find a balance between price and service which is fair for everyone. How should we do this?'

A good remit passes the 'barista test': anyone sharing a coffee can hear it and understand what is required. Confusion and ambiguity must be avoided, so language should be kept simple. Good remits give citizens the freedom to have their say, rather than boxing them in. Open questions that allow participants to consider creative or aspirational answers tend to be more useful than narrow questions. The more information a government can get from a deliberative group of citizens, the more valuable the process for everyone.

As an example, consider these two remits on the same topic: 'Should we build a second airport?' and 'How should we meet our air travel needs?' The first narrows the decision to a yes or no decision on a second airport. With the latter remit, it's likely that participants will make recommendations on a second airport, but they're also given room to make recommendations on all manner of air-travel decisions. This is more useful for everyone, as it neither constrains the community's involvement in the problem, nor limits the extent of valuable advice they can provide to decision-makers.

Remits are very important for a deliberation, as this is not just a simple consultation exercise where communities are asked for input or feedback. Minipublics are addressing real challenges and must provide viable recommendations. Of course, one of the impediments to a viable remit may be that a decision-maker doesn't want to acknowledge a problem. This is a key qualifier for a project from the outset: can the elected representative genuinely say that there's a problem? Participants may need to interpret for themselves what the remit is asking, what aspects need to be addressed, and how this will shape any solutions. This is an opportunity for the group to seek clarity regarding what they are making a decision on – and what is off-limits.

Time is critical too. Without sufficient time, participants will not be able to hear enough evidence, or find agreement, and may even perceive this restriction as a deliberate choice. Ideally, deliberative processes take around three to six months from beginning to end – more if you're embarking on a larger national project. Some topics will be less complex than others, and more suitable to shorter lengths of time. Complexity can be managed by altering the remit, reducing the scope to narrow the breadth of content – but still it's necessary to identify the edges of the box.

Normally, minipublic meetings are roughly the length of a working day. An introductory meet-and-greet evening would allow participants get to know one another socially, before they move into full-day sessions. What matters is that participants have enough face-to-face and online time to ask lots of questions, to receive and think about answers, to discuss things (both among themselves and with experts), to explore information, to form recommendations and to write their report. A program might have four three-hour sessions plus two full days and still find the right balance between information, exploration, deliberation and recommendations. The important factor is that citizens feel sufficiently informed, have had enough opportunity to discuss the issues, and have ownership of their ultimate recommendations.

* * *

When we're thinking about the *who*, we often assume that the more, the better. Right? Wrong. First, it would be an immense, if not impossible task for a huge slice of the community to be involved in a single, quality deliberative process. Second, and more importantly, a large group doesn't actually produce a better outcome than a smaller group. Why is that? More people might mean more precise diversity, but the larger the group, the less incentive there is for individuals to do thorough work – and the more difficult the group is to facilitate. When you're one of 50 people working together, you're motivated to take more responsibility than if you're one of 150, where you can coast along.

We often equate large numbers with political legitimacy. However, a minipublic derives its legitimacy from its equitable representation (the democratic lottery). The minipublic needs to be large enough to capture a wide descriptive diversity, while also being small enough that the participants can invest themselves in the process. We need to resist the instinctive desire to equate size with validity. A smaller number of participants creates the right environment to take advantage of enough differing views and life experiences. For this reason, small groups of stratified random samples can, surprisingly, make better strategic decisions than groups of experts, because cognitive diversity trumps narrow sector ability.[10]

Once we've decided on how many, we must make a decision on the specific *who*. We will need to challenge our instincts and carefully think through who is needed as participants. The hurdle to clear is that most public participation involves a familiar type of citizen, someone in possession of the right combination of time and motivation. It's great to have passionate people in our communities, as they contribute to the vibrancy of our public space, but they do sometimes crowd out the voices of others. What we're hoping to achieve with a minipublic is a descriptive balance: everyone in the community should see someone like themselves involved.

Democratic lotteries and similar selection methods don't claim to find the perfect statistical match. It's technically quite a feat to put together a perfect sample when distilling a national or even state population into a group that can fit in a room. Rounding down until you reach a manageable size will always involve a level of compromise that can be tough to negotiate. Instead, our aim is to arrive at a mix of citizens that finds a descriptive match to the population, and that can consistently be done with groups of 30 to 40 people.

We need to consider a few other factors when deciding on size, one of which is the scale of the decision. Is this a local, regional, state or federal issue? Anything that covers broad geographic distances, or areas that have acutely different experiences of the problem, may warrant two or more separate mini-publics. One example here is a project that concerned future infrastructure spending across a state. The project ran two distinct citizens' juries, one metropolitan and one regional. Operating two different juries allowed the government to hear informed recommendations that were heavily situated within their geographic contexts. National conversations will almost always include more than one group of participants, in order to capture the experiences of the entire country. How many groups, and where, will depend on the problem and how differently it manifests across the country.

When thinking about the scale of a minipublic, the geographical or experiential diversity will help inform whether to facilitate groups apart from one another, before bringing them together for a final decision. Physical distance, the number of people impacted by a decision and the differing ways communities experience an issue are all relevant. A large city, for example, requires a broad strategic plan for its future growth: it has three distinct regions, so forming minipublics in each of these areas separately may be useful, before the groups convene for a final set of meetings.

Since we're explicitly not seeking to involve as many people as possible, we must think carefully about the types of people who should be part of the discussion. On the face of it, the answer is simple: everyone. We should opt for a range of categories that, broadly, offers everyone in the community a fair chance of participating. What makes this challenging is the fairness criterion. Our design decisions will need to walk a tightrope between adapting to the norms of affirmative action for minorities, on the one hand, and the incontrovertible even-handedness of a democratic lottery. Will people think the process was fair if we oversample for minor populations, and the minipublic delivers a result that favours a minority at the expense of the majority, whatever the rationale provided?

There are some occasions where you might want to hear from a specific part of the community on a topic that impacts them uniquely, perhaps on something location-specific, or you need specific youth involvement in solutions that impact them more than others. 'Representation' in the minipublic process isn't limited to its membership. In fact, it's best not to rely on that as the sole measure for including diverse perspectives on any given topic.

Instead, throughout the process, experts, government, key stakeholders and members of the public will offer contributions to help inform, guide and enrich the deliberations of those lucky enough to be selected. On issues where it's important that the participants hear from minority groups, we'll make sure those advocates are given the time and opportunity to contribute meaningfully. This means that various perspectives are all provided with the public legitimacy that they deserve. All voices have a role to play in an assignment that emphasises respect for a diversity of views.

Returning to the parameters of our democratic lottery, simple demographic filters such as age, gender, location and education should be used to stratify the random sample to descriptively represent the community's broad demographics. Ideally, we're mapping these numbers to the most recent census profile of the community, or to the next best dataset. We can use more filters, but only while also keeping in mind the balancing act. Over-engineering who's in the room can lead to accusations of 'fixing' the democratic lottery, or of having too much control over its 'random' nature. At worst, actively 'excluding' people can undermine trust in the process.

There is some debate here. This is to do with the issue of discursive representation. Discursive representation accounts for the thoughts and views in the room. What we've proposed so far has been descriptive representation: the 'look' of the room. While the room might look like the wider community, there could be an undersampling of people who feel a certain way about an issue, and an oversampling of those who have other views. As mentioned above, the way in which views are 'represented' is not limited to those of the participants directly. Special effort is made to offer the group a range of contributions that maximises the diversity of knowledge and experience. This means including any perspectives popularly held in the community, as well as ensuring that minority populations have clear avenues to influence deliberations.

Why, then, would we need to include parameters that ask for participants' views on an issue? The only workable answer is that it can help build trust in the process. Those sceptical of a minipublic might believe that people who give up their time to be part of a lottery will typically be those whose views lean in a certain direction, and so that their position might be over-represented in the final group. It's hard to see this happening with something like a local council budget, but easier to imagine for those responding to a democratic lottery for a national assembly on an issue such as climate change

The challenge with selection by way of a discursive approach is that most people often do not actually know what their view is on a given issue until they've been given time to think about it. We're not all good at reflecting on our prior and unconscious biases, and it's unfair to think everyone has well-thought-out positions on everything. In fact, experts hardly have the time to be informed even on issues adjacent to their own field. This is why we recommend that discursive parameters are used sparingly, and only when they contribute to some much-needed public trust in a process that seriously requires it.

We have only one exception to our rule of non-exclusion: anyone who is in political office, or actively involved in the decision-making of government, should be ineligible for participation. The reason for this is self-evident: it protects against government control or manipulation of the process in an optical and substantive sense. This ensures that government has an observational presence in the room, without playing a role in shaping the outcomes. People are rightly cynical of any attempt to adjust, steer or exert influence over a process.

*　*　*

We've made some decisions on *who*, *how* and *what*. We now need to put some more thought into the *what*: the information to be considered through-out the citizens' journey from innocent bystanders to well-informed decision-makers. Because there's time – and there must be – we can indulge the participants to consider as much information as they like, from all sides of the issue. This is because they'll be in an environment that allows them to study all the evidence slowly and thoroughly.

What, then, do we need to think about when compiling the information and contacting experts for our lucky participants? Like all of these design decisions, the perceived legitimacy and trust in the process should be at the front of our minds. Not only do we need to ensure that a wide range of information is shared, but people watching on need to have faith that the views they hold have been presented fairly and considered by the participants. The participants also need to be equipped with sufficient information to make educated recommendations.

With all of this in mind, there are three key sources of information. The first is the background information kit produced by government. Preparing this can be a huge task. The aim is that the kit clearly shares the problem, that it sets out all the required background information to understand the current approaches, challenges, options, participants and responsibilities, and that it does so in plain language. It's the first means of giving participants a comprehensive starting point, answering as many questions as possible and providing a foundation for their future conversations. The more thorough the information provided, the more time will be saved when the participants are at work in the room.

Information and judgement are required in equal parts to reach considered decisions, and while the judgement of everyday people has been shown to earn very high levels of public trust, it's important that the way information is provided does not erode that trust. This means that information provided to participants cannot be a brochure of government successes – or, even worse, marketing that aims to secure a certain result.

Next, a clear role needs to be provided for key stakeholders and members of the community who wish to contribute. This is the opportunity we spoke about before, so it's important that it is robust and transparent for all. Sometimes establishing a steering group that includes key stakeholders can provide quality insight on what will earn trust in the process. With or without a steering group, though, public submissions from key stakeholders and the wider community are needed to round out perspectives on the topic. Everyone should be invited to submit their views in written form, at least. Asking people to provide their own response to the question, as well as any information they think the group will need to consider, can also be useful. Key experts, industry and community stakeholders and others can, with the help of the steering group, be identified to make contributions in the room. These speakers will be joined by government speakers, in what serves as an opportunity for the participants to engage in some thorough questioning.

Finally, it's important that the participating citizens have control over what information they do and do not receive. This is fundamental to building trust, and also allows the participants to fill gaps in their knowledge with sources of information they rely on. To do this, we'll ask: 'What do you need to know, and who do you trust to inform you?' Importantly, we'll ask this on a few occasions to ensure participants are able to uncover new information as they learn. Not all information requires an in-person speaker; a useful distinction is that often quantitative information can be answered specifically and in writing, while qualitative responses are better given in person and explored through questioning (though this is not a hard and fast rule).

*   *   *

A number of smaller decisions will be made further down the track, but for the time being the next big decision we'll need to make is what the final recommendations report will look like, and who will write it. Our one piece of advice here is that the citizens themselves write the report in its entirety, in any way they like, unedited by anyone else (including the facilitating team, the oversight team and government staff). This is because an unedited report lends significant authenticity to the final set of recommendations, which increases its popular legitimacy as a product of everyday people (compared to polished consultants' documents). This freedom also gives the participants the assurance that they can say whatever they would like: it reinforces their autonomy. It's okay if the report is a bit rough around the edges – this is part of the charm. Success here is measured in participant ownership of the final details and the implementation of their recommendations, not how easy the report is on the eye. Like all the design decisions, the primary motivation is to build public trust in the process.

The report with the final recommendations needs to be made public immediately. This is to protect against cynicism and any lingering lack of trust in the process. The government needs to accept the document and restate its commitment to responding or implementing the recommendations. A more detailed response document needs to follow, in due course, detailing an official governmental position on each recommendation. This closes the loop for the participants and makes it publicly clear that the government has kept its commitment.

In addition to closing the loop, we're also responsible for raising public awareness of both the decision and the role that everyday people played in making it. It's best that this starts before the report has been handed in, so that the public can buy into the process before there is any hint of where it might lead. In this way, the community builds trust in the participants and the process, and not just the report. A good way to achieve this is through video interviews with participants to capture their 'journey', which helps to underline two important aspects. First, that they are everyday people. And second, that they have spent time learning and talking with one another before arriving at a common-ground decision of their own accord.

The communications job is thus to bring the public's attention to this noble undertaking: fellow citizens have worked diligently together for several weeks to achieve an equitable outcome for the community. The ultimate indication of success is when the final report wins the confidence of the broader public.

B

B Is for Belgium

THESE DAYS, WHEN PEOPLE THINK OF *Belgium*, words like *bureaucracy* and *Brexit* also spring to mind. The multicultural achievements of this polyglot country are smothered by its reputation for red tape. However, in July 2018, to the surprise of many, and especially Belgians themselves, this shoehorned little state defeated Brazil in the quarter-finals of the World Cup. I happened to be there – not in Brussels, but in a small town a two-hour train ride east. The place erupted into a red-chemise, beer-swilling, all-night party.

Not many know that Belgium has real democratic pedigree. It was the first country in the world to institute compulsory voting, with Australia a runner-up. The Belgian Constitution of 1831 also provided the template for many other countries, in Europe and in Latin America. Eupen – the small town where I was – is the capital of the German-speaking Ostbelgien community and, like the Dutch-speaking Flanders to the north and the French-speaking Walloon to the south, has its own parliament.

In 2017, the Ostbelgien parliament tasked a citizens' jury with reviewing and making recommendations on the provision of childcare in the region. Following a successful process and outcome, the parliament decided to study whether a more enduring minipublic arrangement could be devised.

The parliament contacted David Van Reybrouck's G1000 organisation, which subsequently recommended convening an international advisory panel. Instructed to design a complementary structure to the existing parliament, the panel proposed a Citizens' Council model, whereby 25 people, selected annually by democratic lottery, would decide on topics for further deliberation by separate citizens' juries. Those juries, each with 25 to 50 people, would discuss the topics in question separately and make recommendations to parliament. A dedicated secretariat would handle all the logistical work.

In February 2019, the Ostbelgien parliament unanimously agreed to go ahead with the model, thus establishing the world's first permanent Citizens' Council, as a complement to the region's elected parliament. The astute reader might suspect that this is typical of Belgium: the introduction of yet another layer of stultifying administration. But this time it was radically different, as it elevated a group of everyday people to the same level as elected politicians.

Decades of research have shown that elected politicians normally come from a very narrow stratum of society. The usual suspects hold university degrees, are male and rarely include younger adults or minorities. Moreover, when politics is professionalised – with elected officials being paid and having no other employment – they're incentivised to stay in office. In Eupen it was different, as the Ostbelgien regional parliament consisted of 25 part-time politicians – all of whom had day jobs – similar to many other local governments around the world, and thus the good burghers of Ostbelgien were more open to change.

Apart from exclusive employment, the Citizens' Council is markedly different to any *elected* legislature – local or otherwise. When people are enlisted for a short period to deliberate on public policies – with no election platform and no inducement for public grandstanding – the structural flaws of elected parliaments are avoided. Firstly, elections are a zero-sum game, as there are only a certain number of seats to win, and so the contest often devolves into cheap point-scoring and tawdry Machiavellian tactics. The fourth American president, James Madison, described political campaigning as 'the vicious arts by which elections are too often carried'.

The second advantage of having a legislature selected by democratic lottery is that the members know they won't be criticised by the media for changing their mind, or for moving away from a 'party line'. By contrast, elections generate animated and divisive political parties, which frustrate consensus building from the get-go. With a Citizens' Council, members will always, of course, bring their own particular views to a subject, but there isn't the branding and siloing that occurs with electoral politics.

With this pioneering reform, it looks like Belgium could be a world beater once again.

3

Oversight and Invitations

W E'VE NOW DONE A CONSIDERABLE amount of work thinking through the design decisions that will shape our minipublic. To make this a reality, though, there's a need to involve some experienced practitioners – people who have worked with minipublics before. It's also important to be clear about how the participants are going to work together, and what their relationship will be with the convening body (often a government agency, parliament or local council). If the citizens are going to invest their time and effort into a complex issue, they need to feel in control.

Having said this, minipublics need management, as the process is unfamiliar to most and doesn't happen organically. A sizeable group will struggle to deliberate without guidance, and having an experienced organisation or individual undertaking operational oversight – being responsible for the delivery of the project from start to finish – helps enormously.

There are two aspects to the oversight role. The first is to maintain participants' trust in the integrity of the process, and the second is to be the intermediary between the participants and the government. The oversight role is ultimately about neutrality, and this can be performed by a university, a judge or an independent nonpartisan organisation such as the newDemocracy Foundation. The vital thing is that whoever is undertaking the role needs to be respected by all sides, and trusted to deliver a fair and impartial process. Usually, those in the oversight role should be distinct from the facilitation team, in order to maintain a truly independent source of scrutiny.

The public are sometimes rightfully cynical of the results consultants deliver because they're paid to complete the task. When designing a minipublic, public perception is paramount and significant issues will be subject to heavier scrutiny, often necessitating oversight that is transparently independent.

While on the topic of trust and oversight – and in keeping with the fundamental tenet of transparency – all local media should be encouraged to witness the process. The bare minimum should be to invite and explain the process to the media, but a more useful approach would be to have journalists interview some participants throughout the process, checking in with the same people to see their changes in view, and to tell something of their personal story. When the community has had the opportunity to 'meet' the participants before a decision is made, the public can better relate to the participants and the process without reference to any particular result or decision. This helps scale the impact, by spreading the idea that people like them are involved in making a big decision on their behalf. Only one thing is asked of the participants when speaking to the media: that they do not forecast results or pre-judge any recommendations before the final report is issued. This is because no decision is conclusive until it has been decided by the entire group, in the form of the final report.

Anyone in the room who is part of neither the facilitation nor the oversight team is designated as an observer. This includes government staff, who have a unique role. There are situations where staff might be best placed to answer off-the-cuff questions arising from participants. Responses here can be polar: sometimes staff are too eager to jump in and give their take on an issue of doubt, but more often than not they are hesitant to respond because they're concerned about providing their personal perspective, which could be construed as 'the government position'. Finding the right balance here is crucial to filling information gaps with agility while retaining the desired 'hands-off' approach by government.

We always defer to the facilitation team for exactly how they'd like to manage the 'ask a staff member' issue. It's about juggling a habit of deferring to staff when participants should be doing their own learning without relying on a single source in the room for clarity, but equally we'd like the participants to have access to the odd quick fact check or taste-test of the impact of a recommendation. We can keep the following adage in mind: government advice is on tap, but not on top.

With citizen control and facilitated involvement in the room, an environment can be created that enables staff to provide real-time fact checks or grounding statements that help participants find their way to their own decisions. The simple rule is that the participants decide when they want to hear from staff, and that staff only act on directions from the facilitator. This means participants can sanity-check the intent and outcome of recommendations to ensure that what they're advising will be interpreted by government in the right way. When this relationship sings, it benefits the final output immensely. And remember, members of the wider public and media will also be in the room, and they too act as a safety check on the fairness and quality of the process, to ensure participants are not being led.

*   *   *

So far, we've done a lot of talking about everything other than how we're actually going to get people in the room for our minipublic assembly. Now let's consider what it's going to take to involve a wide range of people who don't normally participate in this type of thing.

Gathering a diverse mix of laypeople requires careful thinking and planning, and the organisers must understand why most people currently say 'no' to community engagement – and why this offer is different. We need to think creatively in order to reach people from all walks of life, and explain to them what is involved, and how their participation might produce positive outcomes for their neighbours.

Democratic lotteries can become technical, but at their most basic they make use of random recruitment to dilute the self-selection bias that normally exists in engagement. It's obvious that we're not going to be able to eliminate this bias, short of mandating participation, and there will always be some who, for whatever reason, cannot participate. Our aim, then, is to design a recruitment model that will reach as many people as possible, and ensure that everyone has a fair chance of participating. We need to make sure we lower the barriers to entry so that it is not difficult for someone to say yes. Relevant measures here include financial reimbursements, catering, offers for travel allowances and perhaps even paid childcare. Ensuring that people feel encouraged to take part is the first challenge, and overcoming it starts with fancy invitations.

Our invitations need to reach a sometimes quite cynical pool of people, and so they have to be of a high standard if they are to survive the walk between the mailbox and the recycling bin. We have only a brief moment to capture people's attention among all the other messages they receive daily. The success of our process relies on the quality of the group we put together, because our democratic lottery is only as good as the pool of applicants we feed into it. We will need to be aggressively realistic in our approach. We must emphasise what we know will incentivise people to open the envelope and what will encourage them to read the contents. What newDemocracy has found is that the more you can convey the uniqueness of the opportunity – and the authority vested in the process – the more likely people are to apply. With this in mind, we're going to make it clear on the front of the invitation exactly how much money people will be paid for their time, and include a statement of the authority given to the process by the minister or mayor.

Some decision-makers shy away from advertising the amount of money paid to participants, perhaps fearing that only those interested in the cash will be attracted, or perhaps because they think it cheapens the seriousness of an issue that ought to attract participants without such a carrot. Whatever the case, a decision to shy away from any incentive for the wider public to participate would be a bad one.

We should then spend the rest of our invitation clearly explaining what the topic is, how people's input will directly help solve the problem, what the process involves and what the time commitment would be. We would also include some motivational text that encourages a sense of innovation and civic obligation. Good invitations require creative design thinking, and because we all collect mail at some point in our week, we all have a sense of what captures our attention (or not). Sometimes the less it looks like regular government engagement material, the better.

We now need to determine who we're going to send our invitations to. If you're creating physical invitations, as is often done, you will require a database of postal addresses. What type of database you need will depend on how we're going to address the invites. Ideally, we're blessed with a complete database that details everyone in the community and their current address. That'll mean we can send personally addressed invitations to a random sample of the population, as personalised mail is significantly more likely to be opened. An electoral database, if it's available, is a good start. It's not often we're fortunate enough to access this database, though, so instead we can opt for a complete database of physical addresses sourced from a national postal service. This will lose the benefit of personalisation but will allow us to sample each household and everyone inside it.

How many invitations are required? It depends on our expected response rate and the total applicant pool we're aiming for. A rough guide is a 1:10 ratio for participants to applicants. This will ensure we have enough people from all demographics so that it's possible to fairly draw an eligible jury. For a jury of 50 people, this will mean we need 500 applicants at a minimum, and to achieve the 500, using a standard response rate of roughly 3 to 5 per cent, equates to between 10,000 and 17,000 invites. Given that we cannot be certain of our response rate (or that all invitations will be successfully delivered and that responses will be adequately uniform across demographics) it's better to send additional invitations. It's much harder to get fresh applicants than it is to send out more invitations. With this in mind, for our 50-person jury, we might opt to send out 20,000 invitations.

If we're not sending physical invitations to addresses at random, we'll need to design a strategy that accounts for the loss of that initial random sampling of addresses. We can use digital invitations in a way that aims to draw in as many people as possible (to dilute the impact of self-selection), offering the invitation to every single person in the community and then conducting our random selection from the pool of people who apply. The crucial factor here is whether we're confident that just about everyone will have seen or heard of the opportunity. If we are, then we can be satisfied that enough people will volunteer to dilute the 'usual suspects' conundrum.

Once we've sent the invitations, we'll need to make it easy for people to RSVP. The easiest method for registering is an online form with a simple URL, so that people can easily complete the relevant demographic information, as well as, of course, their name, address and contact details. Another option is to include a mail-in form with the physical invitation, which allows people to post back their RSVP, and a telephone number so that respondents can call or send an SMS if they prefer. As with other design decisions, the aim here is to make it as easy as possible for someone to go from curious about the process to all signed up, with their fingers crossed that they'll be selected in the draw.

Now to the lottery. To do this, there's newDemocracy's free online tool[11]. This will randomly select an eligible jury that matches the desired demographic stratification and ensures that everyone has a fair chance of being selected. Anyone can access this open-source and publicly available tool.

Once we've conducted our lottery, those who are selected are contacted by an email seeking confirmation in writing of their desire to participate. Each participant will also be contacted by phone prior to the first meeting. This is an opportunity for the organiser to encourage a strong personal commitment to participating, as once the process is underway, it's difficult to backfill for non-attendees. Often it is too difficult for late additions to catch up with the learning and deliberating the group has already done. We'll therefore over-recruit for our initial sample, knowing that sometimes people have to withdraw from what might be a three-month-long process. Our phone call will cover all the usual onboarding – dates, questions, logistics – but we'll also endeavour to ask some personal questions around why the participant said yes, and what their hopes are for the process. These questions build a relationship between the participant and the organiser, building confidence in the process and a stronger commitment to attend.

This recruitment model is a little tricky – it takes time to get it right, and requires considerable resources when compared to standard community engagement practices. But there's a good reason. The success of any minipublic hinges on whether or not the wider community really do see people like themselves in the room, and trust the selection process. The reward for this rigorous recruitment methodology is getting that seemingly preposterous 'mirror image' of the population at large – and when it happens, the feeling in the room is formidable. After finding and convincing people to take the time to participate, it's now over to them do the hard work of learning, deliberating and reaching agreement.

C Is for Cottonopolis, COVID and Climate Change

I N JANUARY 2020, PRE-COVID, I VISITED Manchester for an International Week of Democratic Innovation. At the beginning of the nineteenth century, Manchester was known as 'Cottonopolis' – it was the world's largest industrial town, with the worst industrial conditions. After direct experience with his own mill there, the German expatriate Friedrich Engels published *The Condition of the Working Class in England*. Three years later, in 1848, Engels joined with Karl Marx to write *The Communist Manifesto*. In the same year, the Chartists presented The People's Charter to the UK parliament. Signed by almost two million people, it called for an extension of voting rights to all men. Both the Whigs and Tories regarded the Chartists as 'enemies of property and public order' and rejected their demands outright.

Where the Chartists failed in England, they succeeded down under. Australia led the world in democratic innovations throughout the nineteenth century, beginning with the secret ballot, the first independent electoral commission, and then compulsory and preferential voting. The United States and the United Kingdom were decades behind these developments. Moreover, both countries still persevere with optional and first-past-the-post voting, even though the outcomes are discernibly inferior. Average voting turnouts in the United States and the United Kingdom are below 65 per cent, compared to Australia's 90 per cent, and the preferential vote clearly provides a more accurate picture of voters' intentions. New Zealand is often heralded as pioneering the vote for women, but it was in Australia that women were first able to stand for office, some twenty years ahead of the Kiwis. The American political scientist Louise Overacker wrote in 1952, 'No modern democracy has shown greater readiness to experiment than Australia.'[12]

At the Manchester conference, the international delegates were all wanting to experiment further, going 'beyond elections' in each of their home countries. Claudia Chwalisz from the Organisation for Economic Co-operation and Development (OECD) presented the *Deliberative Wave* report, which recommended that citizens' assemblies be embedded into democratic institutions.

After Manchester, I returned to Australia, at the time that COVID took hold across the globe. The world was catapulted into a health crisis: the medical advice informed the political directives, which the public generally complied with. But despite the turmoil caused by the virus, more people still considered the climate crisis as big a threat as COVID. An April 2020 Ipsos poll conducted in fourteen countries found that two-thirds of people believed environmental issues were as serious as the pandemic, and wanted their governments to prioritise climate action as part of the economic recovery.[13] In 2019, the French government had already initiated a Citizens' Assembly on environmental issues, which we in Manchester had followed with keen interest. In July 2020, at the conclusion of that assembly's deliberations, President Emmanuel Macron announced a €15 billion program in response to the Assembly's Report.

The French Citizens' Assembly was composed of 150 people selected by-lot. Invitations to participate had been sent to 70,000 randomly generated telephone numbers with this message:

The Citizens' Convention on Climate announced by President Emmanuel Macron is organised by the Economic, Social and Environmental Council. The objective of this Convention is to go further and faster in the fight against climate change, and to give more space to citizen participation in public decision-making. For better representation, it was decided that the participants be chosen by drawing lots. Your telephone number is one of those drawn at random, and we give you the opportunity to participate. In principle, do you agree to participate in this Citizens' Convention on Climate?

For the pool who agreed to participate, a stratified demographic crosscheck was made for the random draw of 150:

- Gender: equal men and women
- Age: proportional from 16 years upwards
- Level of education and socioeconomic: welfare recipients, without qualifications, blue-collar and white-collar employees, and managers
- Residency and geography: major urban centres, outer suburbs and rural municipalities.

The 150 participants deliberated for six months, having divided into five thematic groups: Transportation, Consumption, Living and Housing, Production and Work, and the Food Sector.

Among the proposals put to government were a reduction of solo car rides and air travel, and a cap on the extension of existing airports. Transportation produces 30 per cent of greenhouse gases. The citizens were also prepared to tax products with a high carbon footprint and low nutritional benefit.

At the end of the presentations, President Macron told the Assembly: 'You have shown that it is possible – on even the most difficult and flammable subject – to create consensus.'

4

Deliberation and Facilitation

WHEN CONSIDERING A MINIPUBLIC, it's useful to think about it in two parts. The first part contains all the planning, the negotiating of authority, the recruitment and the administrative work to set the process in motion. The second part is when the ball gets rolling: a group of strangers meets for the first time, deliberation begins and the process unfolds along a loosely determined path that results in common-ground recommendations. Until now, this book has been focusing on the first part of the process. In this final chapter we'll cover what is expected of our participants, and how they'll be helped along their path from discovery and learning to agreement and action. This ultimately begins with distinguishing deliberation from other types of discussion, and how this specific approach to solving a problem as a group can lead to surprising and incisive recommendations.

This is one of those parts of the process where we can allow ourselves to feel inspired. We have now realised the ideal environment for a mix of people in conversation who have a shared purpose. We see hundreds of ideas cast across the wall on post-it notes. Young participants are helping their old colleagues through the nuances of technology, others are talking about their community while catching some respite over a cup of tea. There are small tables of people considering information in depth, hearing differing perspectives and critically analysing different ways of thinking. There is an overwhelming sense of togetherness in deliberation, because of the way it frames the conversation amongst neighbours working together to find agreement. When we're free from that anchoring bias of trying to win an argument or defeat an idea, we can slow down, listen to one another and reach that fabled common ground.

Here, we are speaking about public deliberation, not the internal deliberation that we each do during our own personal contemplation. We're not talking about debate either. Debate might occur when there is an invited panel of experts arguing their various positions. While debate has a role to play in a sort of 'competition of ideas', deliberation is distinctively different. This is because the aim of a public deliberation is to investigate various options by hearing from experts, exploring common ground and finally reaching a group decision. The fundamental difference between deliberation and debate is whether the end objective is either win/lose or consensus seeking.

Any social group tends to be dominated by 'Type A' personalities – the confident orators. They are often charismatic and persuasive, but there's a need to keep them in check, so as to allow others the space to have their say. To do this, we'll ask the group to draft their own guidelines for how they'll respectfully engage in considerate but robust discussion.

We'll also encourage small groups of five to six, so everyone has the chance to have their say. Small groups also allow for a diversity of voices to emerge, and closer relationship building. Also, because we all tend to sit with people like us, it's good to have to converse with someone we might normally never talk to. Working in small groups ensures that participants are less likely to accidentally or intentionally form cliques. Sometimes people don't get along, or they may be unproductive when working in the same group, so mixing up the groups keeps things energised and allows different social styles and demographics to be evenly distributed. Having a good blend of task-based and people-based social styles will help the group to stick to its timetables, while also going into detail.

Setting different tasks for small groups can enable the minipublic to explore large quantities of information at the same time. Small groups can also generate and refine many ideas simultaneously.

This deliberative process is *not* a natural enterprise – and it's certainly not obvious in our partisan political system. That's because it requires skilful facilitation – just enough support to allow the group to make its own decisions and find its own way, and not so much that it interferes. However, when the going gets tough, the facilitator can keep the group working well.

Our minipublic involves professional facilitators who have the experience to deliver from start to finish, in a transparent, collaborative, independent and respectful manner that ultimately works to empower the group. The facilitator's role begins with contributing to the design of the process. They'll act as an adviser on all the key decisions, including the number of days, the number of participants and even the remit of the minipublic. This is because they're responsible for delivering the deliberation. A bad outcome is when design decisions are made without facilitator involvement, and the minipublic ends up being impractical, dysfunctional or both.

Deliberative processes require a different type of shepherding that has a light touch, but is also task-driven. We're striking a balance between ensuring that everyone feels warm, welcome and comfortable in offering their view, and keeping them on track so they complete the job to the deadline.

We'll make use of exercises designed to challenge cognitive biases and test expert knowledge, because the group will be weighing up various contested options. They'll need to challenge their own assumptions, as well as think carefully about the sources of the information and competing claims they are being presented with. The group members will establish their own agreed behavioural guidelines, setting criteria for gathering information, testing it, brainstorming solutions, prioritising those possibilities, agreeing on recommendations and accounting for minority opinions when a consensus is not found – and for collectively writing the report.

The work will be enjoyable, and often arduous, but the group will feel a tremendous sense of collective achievement once the mission is accomplished.

There are different ways of describing the journey that participants make through a process; we like to show this graphic to neatly tell the story. The traditional approach to engagement is captured at the beginning, as *Business as Usual*. Our approach takes much longer, and involves distinct phases that explain what the group is doing at each point of the process.

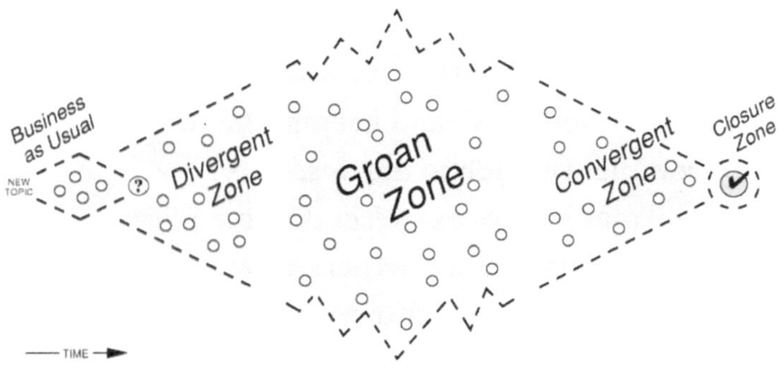

From **Facilitator's Guide to Participatory Decision-Making,**
by Sam Kaner et al. (*Jossey-Bass, San Francisco, 2014*)

The first phase of the deliberation is when all the available information is reviewed – the *Divergent Zone*. Participants are given the freedom to explore the topic at their own pace. They will interrogate information, ask questions, receive answers and ask follow-up questions. This stage is all about casting the net both wide and deep. The breadth of sources is as important as the detail of the responses. Participants are also provided an opportunity to ask questions of key decision-makers who are giving their authority to the process. This is an important step to build trust. They will ask questions like: Why are you undertaking this process? What will you do with our recommendations? How can we trust that you will not go back on your word?

The second phase is the aptly titled *Groan Zone*. This is the constant back-and-forth of gathering information and making sense of it all. Some participants will always want more information, but the challenge is to begin to understand and articulate where the process is heading. At some point, the group will need to stop accumulating information, and start condensing their knowledge and generating ideas. The participants will be reminded that the aim is to become informed citizens, not subject experts. This is difficult, and there is a risk that the process might be derailed if not managed properly.

The third phase is the *Convergent Zone*. The aim here is for the group to be clear about *what* they would like to happen, and *why*. We will ask them to communicate the *why* because it ensures that the community and the decision-maker understand the reasoning behind their recommendations, and can then flexibly apply this reasoning to other aspects of the issue, now and in the future. Strict recommendations that focus on the *how* can restrict problem-solving by being inflexible when circumstances change.

Coming up with ideas can be easy for some groups and hard for others. We'll need to keep reminding the group to focus on the clarity of their intent. It needs to be easy for someone reading the recommendations to understand what the group is asking for, and why. We're also going to encourage the group to avoid wish-list recommendations that do not factor in trade-offs. Idea-generating exercises need to start broad. People are going to be encouraged to disagree and come up with competing ideas. Once this phase is passed, there's no going back to fresh ideas generation. If this is not made clear, and someone misses an opportunity to present their idea, we risk losing the trust of the group.

Once the group has generated ideas, they can combine and even aggregate recommendations in themes. Logically organising recommendations into topics or themes can give the final report a clearer narrative. This whole convergent zone is about finding common ground around ideas that the group can live with. We'll place a strong emphasis on where the bar is for including a recommendation in the final report – somewhere around 80 per cent support within the group. This ensures that the recommendations in the report are those that the community can all broadly support, and not competing recommendations with simple majorities. The latter, clearly, would result in an incoherent report.

The last phase is the *Closure Zone*. This is all about agreeing on and writing the final set of recommendations, and concluding the process. The writing instructions will be quite simple. Focus on precise language and clarity of intent. Writing up recommendations is an iterative process. Recommendations start as basic ideas, to which detail is slowly added. This means that at each point, the group can reflect on and add clarity to the purpose of a recommendation.

The task of writing a report that can be supported by the group requires parallel work. Participants will need to split up, refine recommendations and ultimately write them into the report at the same time. There are different methods for this, but most use templates that ensure each recommendation has the same format.

The picture we're painting here is a room full of small working groups clustered around laptops, young paired with old. They're writing from notes they've developed in the larger group, and are delegating the detailed work on each recommendation to others because of the good faith which the process has built.

Coming to agreement on what is and is not in the final report requires the whole group to test the recommendations with one another. Different methods can be used to do this, such as is putting the proposals up on a wall, for individual voting with dot stickers. In reviewing the report, the group asks itself what has to change for it to get the requisite support. At this point, the group need not worry about grammar and tiny mistakes; the intent is to capture whether or not each recommendation has support, not the way the recommendation is written. This process can be quite dynamic, with participants moving around, canvassing what changes could bring more people over the physical line in the room. Sometimes all that is missing is a technicality; sometimes more clarity is needed. Sometimes, of course, people just cannot quite find the right amount of agreement.

One of the best ways to test the recommendations, if there is time, is to pass them to the decision-maker and get feedback. This is most useful when the decision-maker can give clear comments on how they interpret each recommendation, and what it would mean if it was implemented. This can only be done at the request of, or with the consent of, the citizens. Some key things to keep in mind are whether or not a recommendation has a high cost or a complex trade-off that may not have been considered, or whether or not a recommendation falls outside the jurisdiction of the decision-maker. If the feedback indicates that a recommendation is not doing what it was intended to do, then it will need to be reworded in a way that captures both the intent of the minipublic and the reason for the recommendation, so that it is not misinterpreted.

There may be recommendations that do not receive enough support to be included in the final report, but that some participants feel decision-makers should nevertheless see. In this case, a minority report can be included. Although not a formal recommendation, this can be useful information for the decision-maker to keep in mind. The minority is not a one-person exercise: no less than 10 per cent of the group should be supporting each point.

Finally, once the recommendations have been agreed upon, the group will be asked to complete the report by writing an introduction that gives a quick narrative of the process. This can be done by a nominated individual or by the group as a collective. When someone picks up the report at the bus stop or a local cafe, he or she should be able to learn from this introduction the basics of the process. Who wrote this report? What was the question? What did they say? Who did they hear from? How did they come to agreement? What do I need to know?

You can see from this whirlwind description of a three-month process that participants will spend much of their time in mixed small-table conversations, while regularly checking in with the whole group and its overall direction. It's a process that can be seen to unfold quite naturally, but at every step there's a risk people will be distracted by new information, competing interests or the timetable. For this reason, we need skilled facilitators to help guide participants, with specially designed exercises built around finding common ground.

This facilitation role involves managing everything that happens 'inside the room': group cohesion, staff input, experts, timekeeping and the actions of the facilitators themselves. They're the pair of hands behind the toddler on the training wheels, helping our participants get to know each other, receive information, understand that information, come up with ideas, and review, prioritise and refine those ideas, all with an eye on how the inputs and the outputs are managed along the way.

Ultimately, the facilitation team is responsible for taking a group from knowing next to nothing about a topic, through a shared learning experience, to making decisions that will shape the future of their community – and doing so in an impartial way. It's as hard – and rewarding – as it sounds.

5

The Future

NOTWITHSTANDING THE MORAL POTENCY of *one person/one vote*, elections are a problem – even the freest and the fairest of them – because they foster divisiveness and glib politics. Where to from here? We strongly believe that minipublics are the future. They address the long-standing existential shortcomings of our current political system, and provide a promising alternative to representative democracy as we know it.

They can be used at the local level to solve the prioritising of thin budgets, or they can be used for long-term constitutional change for the country. In short, they can make for better parliaments, and better democracy.

However, minipublics, on their own, without authority, and in isolation from wider public input, lack the political legitimacy that makes them powerful. And when many pressing issues are seen to require fast and decisive action, they can be regarded as being too cumbersome. But we must be realistic about good processes, which underpin beneficial long-term change.

As trust in politics continues to fall, so too does the belief that our institutions can do anything to arrest their own decline. The universal franchise – so valiantly championed by the working poor – is now a poisoned apple. People may be turned off by the mendacity of politics, but they still vote, through gritted teeth. What other options do they have?

The prize of democracy lies beyond elections.

Cats in the Sack

I WAS FORTUNATE TO HAVE BEEN INVITED as a panellist on ABC-TV's *Q&A* program a couple of times. We had badgered the producer, Peter McEvoy, about getting a run on the show, and he and the host at the time, Tony Jones, generously obliged us. Iain got a run as well. The format regularly featured politicians arguing for or against a particular issue; and a Twitter scroll – with comments from the public at the bottom of the screen – livened things up. The show was often engaging and provocative, with some episodes attracting an audience of close to a million.

For my first appearance, in June 2015, I was privileged to join a panel of distinguished guests: Gillian Triggs, Noel Pearson, Bret Walker, and the Speaker of the House of Representatives, Bronwyn Bishop. It was a special episode, broadcast live from the Great Hall at Parliament House in Canberra, on the 800th anniversary of the signing of the Magna Carta.

I didn't appreciate it at the time but I was, in reality, a bit of a ring-in. Tony Jones gave everyone the opportunity to reflect on the importance of the Magna Carta, and Noel Pearson, the only Indigenous Australian on the panel, said that 'of all of the miserable cargo that came out of the British Isles, there were three very beautiful things: Earl Grey's tea, that sublime game cricket and the common law of England'. Pearson and the other guests were all from the legal profession, and so when my turn came, I admitted to being only a 'bush lawyer', and said that '… for me the Magna Carta at its heart refers to judgments by one's peers'.

Later in the show, I had a little clash with Bronwyn Bishop, who said, 'I believe in free enterprise and individualism, and if I believed in collectivism, I would've joined the other side.' I chose to counter that with: 'I don't think the community at large necessarily relates to the fossilised relics of those ideological positions.' That got a big laugh!

In 2020, as COVID-19 spread across the globe, Australia's Liberal/National coalition government – the supposed champion of small government – launched Australia's biggest ever peacetime spending program. How did they reconcile this with their laissez-faire principles? They argued that Labor would have been more reckless with their spending, and they pointed to Labor's record during the global financial crisis.

Political parties continue to manufacture their differences, even as their political ideologies evaporate. It's not the politicians' fault: it's the system we've all signed up to – the one Churchill infamously described as 'the worst form of government, except for all those others that have been tried from time to time'.

On another occasion on *Q&A*, in February 2017, the four other guests with me on the panel were James Paterson, a federal Liberal MP; Jacqui Lambie, an Independent senator from Tasmania; Kate Ellis, a federal Labor MP; and Yassmin Abdel-Magied, an outspoken advocate for minorities. Tony Jones, again the host, asked: 'Luca, today, in a joint statement, eighteen groups, including the Business Council of Australia, all the way through to the Council of Social Services, called for an end to political finger-pointing and partisanship. How would you actually go about doing that? Can you literally take big decisions out of the parliament?'

I replied: 'I think the problem with the parliament now, it's a bit like cats in a sack. We might think, "Let's put a more clever cat into the sack," thinking that that might resolve things. And what we forget is, actually, the problem is the sack. You know? So, how can we actually provide a more collaborative space? I mean, that's what we're trying to do with this parliament, because now, whatever happens here, there seems to be this cheap point-scoring, one-upmanship. We've got to try and get away from this. I think most Australians, the public, is just frustrated and exasperated with this unproductive bickering. Can we not do something better?'

Later on, Tony then asked me: 'How would you do it better?'

My response: 'I think the most underused asset in politics today is the common sense of everyday people, not when they vote, but when they deliberate together. Not when they're debating, but when they have no incentive to win the debate.

'The experience that we have around the world now, in the last ten years or so, with these citizen juries – not just here in Australia – in Ireland they had a constitutional convention made up of 99 people, 66 of whom were randomly recruited. People are recognising, governments are recognising, that a way to resolve some of these wicked problems is to take the politics out of it, and bring the public into the middle of the room, let them hear from the so-called domain experts, the sector professionals, and let them deliberate and come to some reasonable conclusions.

'And invariably that happens.'

Notes

1   *Q&A*, ABC-TV, 26 March 2018.

2   See, www.democracyrd.org.

3   OECD, *Innovative Citizen Participation and New Democratic Institutions: Catching the Deliberative Wave*, OECD Publishing, Paris, 2020.

4   David Van Reybrouck, *Against Elections: The Case for Democracy*, Bodley Head, London, 2016.

5   Kofi Annan, 'The Crisis of Democracy', speech at the 2017 Athens Democracy Forum, 13 September 2017, www.kofiannanfoundation.org/supporting-democracy-and-elections-with-integrity/athens-democracy-forum.

6   George Tridimas, 'Democracy without Political Parties: The Case of Ancient Athens', *Journal of Institutional Economics*, Cambridge University Press, 2019.

7   Ari Berman, 'How Endangered Is American Democracy?, *The New York Times*, 13 April 2018, www.nytimes.com/2018/04/13/books/review/steven-levitsky-daniel-ziblatt-how-democracies-die.html.

8   David Van Reybrouck, 'Letters to the Editor', *The New York Times*, 4 May 2018, www.nytimes.com/2018/05/04/books/review/letters-to-the-editor.html.

9   Daniel Kahnneman, *Thinking, Fast and Slow*, Farrar, Straus & Giroux, New York, 2011.

10 Hélène Landemore, 'Deliberation, Cognitive Diversity, and Democratic Inclusiveness: An Epistemic Argument for the Random Selection of Representatives', *Synthese*, vol. 190, 2013, pp. 1209–31.

11 See, selection.newdemocracy.com.au.

12 Louise Overacker, *The Australian Party System*, Yale University Press, 1952.

13 'Two Thirds of Citizens Around the World Agree Climate Change Is as Serious a Crisis as Coronavirus', *Ipsos*, 22 April 2020, www.ipsos.com/en/two-thirds-citizens-around-world-agree-climate-change-serious-crisis-coronavirus.

About the authors

Luca Belgiorno-Nettis is the Managing Director of Transfield Holdings, and Prisma Investment – a private family office. In 2004 he founded the newDemocracy Foundation, a non-for-profit research organisation focused on political reform. In 2009 he was awarded an AM for his work in arts and the community generally, and in 2014 he was awarded an Honorary Doctorate from Western Sydney University.

Kyle Redman is the Research and Design Program Manager at the newDemocracy Foundation. He is an internationally recognised expert on minipublics. His research into deliberative democracy and real-world experimentation seeks to challenge how we 'do democracy'.

www.ingramcontent.com/pod-product-compliance
Lightning Source LLC
Chambersburg PA
CBHW031351060726
47590CB00007B/2724